CONTENTS

WHAT IS TECH?

Technology, or 'tech', is all around us: it's in our homes, it's on the street, it's in hospitals, it allows us to travel and communicate with each other. But what actually is it?

Tech is the **products** or **tools** humans create to solve problems and make life easier. Phones, computers, TVs, cars, lights, washing machines and cameras are all tech. So are the apps that allow you to listen to music, play games, find your route on a map or send messages to friends and family.

MONDAY 25
10:00

NEW
WAT

VR SET
249.99

LINE
A B C

MONDAY 25
10:00

BUY
NOW

4 NEWS

A **tech start up,** also known as a company is a group of people who work together to create tech products. To be successful, they must create something that a lot of people want or need.

DID YOU KNOW?
Someone who launches their own start-up is often called an **entrepreneur.**

While you're reading this book, **new types of technology** are being invented! That's the exciting thing about tech – it is always changing, and new types are always being created.

WHY DO
WE NEED TECH?

Imagine a world with no tech at all . . .

How long would it take you to travel to the next town or city? What would you do to speak to someone quickly on the other side of the world? Where would you go if you broke a bone and there were no X-ray machines? We don't need tech to do everything. But it can help us live better, longer, happier lives. And it is a crucial part of almost everyone's jobs . . .

Doctors and **dentists** need computers to store information about their patients as well as machines to take a closer look at their body or teeth and prescribe the right medicine.

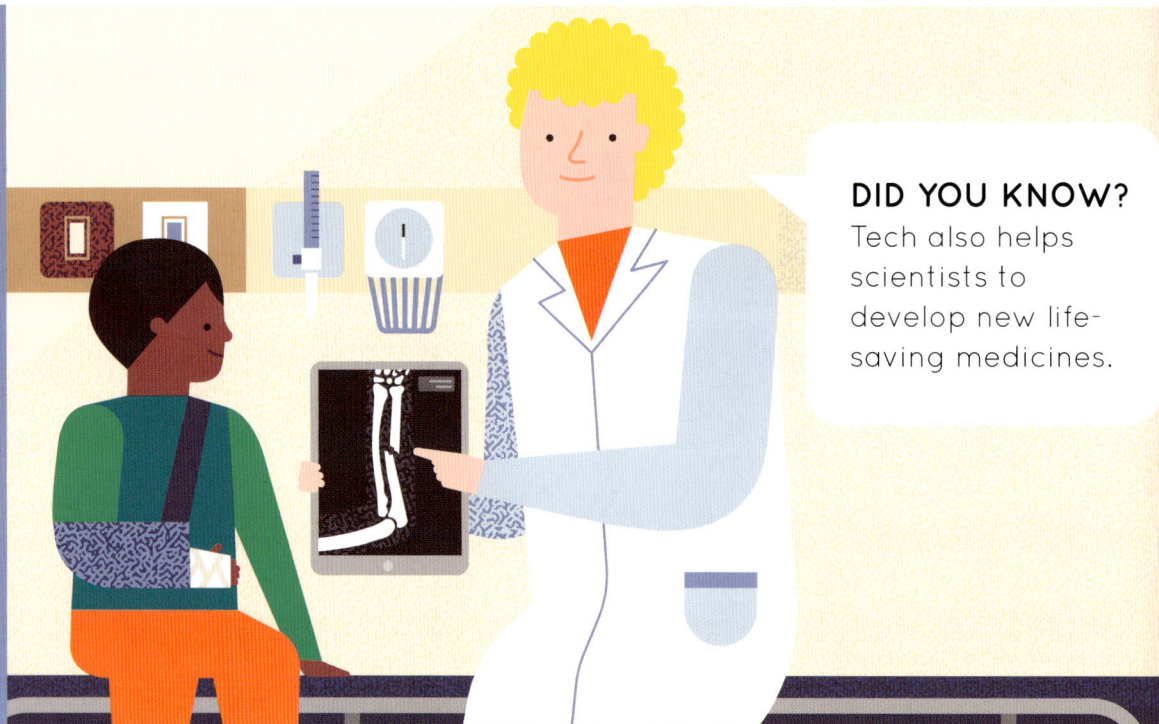

DID YOU KNOW?
Tech also helps scientists to develop new life-saving medicines.

Farmers need vehicles, tools and sometimes robots on their farms to help them grow and pick their crops.

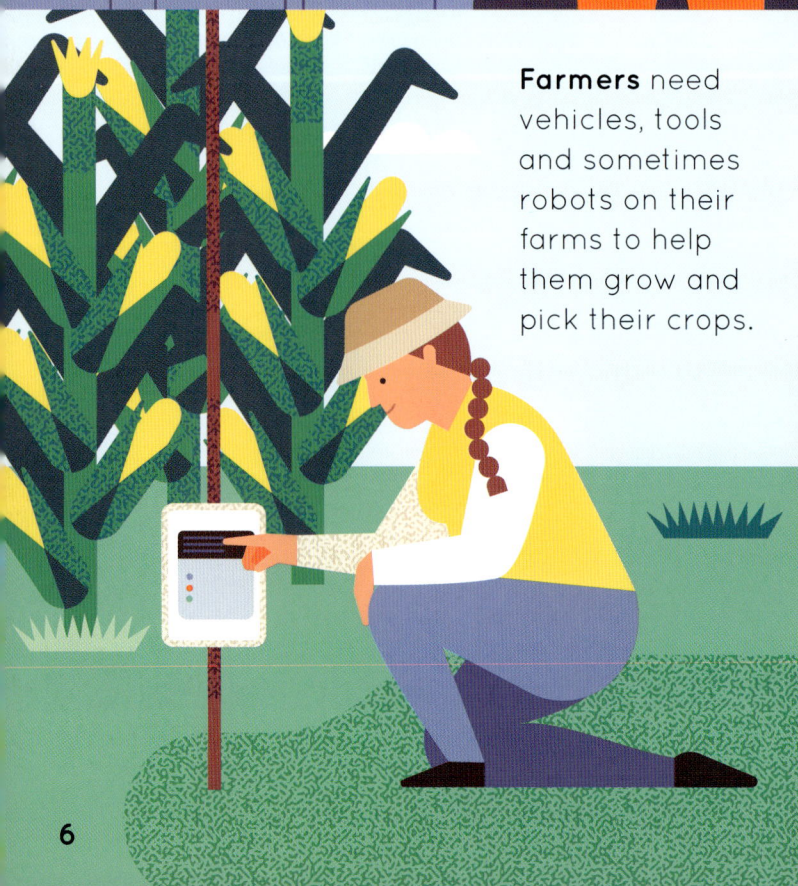

Police officers need security cameras to solve crimes, computers to store information (or 'data') and phones or radios to communicate with each other quickly in emergencies.

CAM 1 CAM 2 CAM 3 CAM 4
CAM 5 CAM 6 CAM 7 CAM 8
CAM 9 CAM 10 CAM 11

Architects, engineers and **builders** need computer programs, tools and even drones to plan and construct buildings.

Banks use computers to store information about how much money people have. Cash machines make it easy for people to get money out, and banking apps let people pay using their phones.

PLEASE SELECT ONE

NOSY BANK
4608 1265 4509
03/20   09/26
Ulysses Smith

Shopkeepers need cash registers and card machines to take payments, as well as security cameras and alarms to keep their shops safe.

Without tech, we wouldn't have animation software to make video games or cartoons. There would be no cameras, videos, TV shows or films.

SCORE
00125

LUCA VS ACER
LEVEL 4

YOU WIN!

Sometimes it's difficult to believe that we didn't always have tech in the world. In fact, much of the tech we use every day was only invented in the last 100 years . . .

THE HISTORY OF
TECH

Humans have been inventing and using tools for thousands of years, but it wasn't that long ago that we started using machines to solve more difficult problems.

French inventor Blaise Pascal invented the Pascaline, a clockwork calculator that could add up to 999,999.

Scottish inventor Alexander Graham Bell invented the telephone.

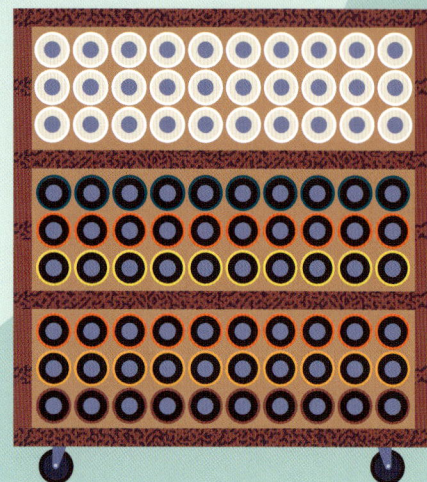

British Alan Turing and American-Hungarian John von Neumann developed the earliest form of computers.

1642	1843	1875	1926	1940s	1953

English mathematician and writer Ada Lovelace wrote the earliest known computer program before computers even existed.

American mathematician Katherine Johnson became a 'human computer' for NASA. Her calculations helped send many astronauts into space.

The world's first television was demonstrated to scientists in London by Scottish engineer John Logie Baird.

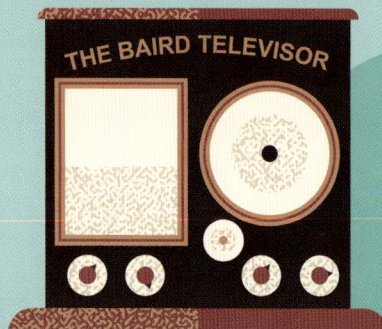

THE BAIRD TELEVISOR

INTERFACE
MESSAGE
PROCESSOR

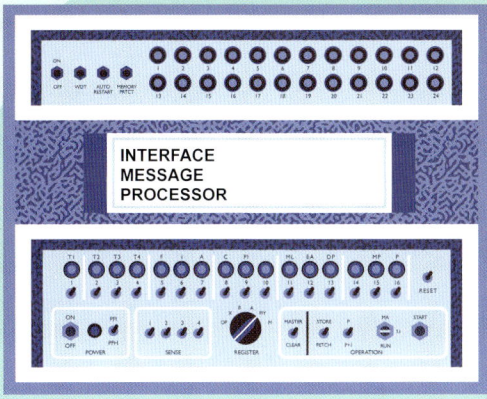

The first computer network (the internet) was invented. It was called ARPANET.

ChatGPT was launched. It is a type of Artificial Intelligence (AI) that can create human-like text.

The World Wide Web was invented by British computer scientist Tim Berners-Lee. It is a system for accessing and navigating the internet.

The first iPhone was created by Apple.

| 1969 | 1980s | 1989 | 1997 | 2007 | 2016 | 2022 |

Handheld games consoles became popular for playing games such as 'Donkey Kong II.'

The first mobile app was created by Nokia. It was a game called 'Snake'.

American robotics designer David Hanson created Sophia, a robot who can take part in conversations and show 60 facial expressions.

HOW DO YOU
FIND YOUR IDEA?

To start a tech company, you need a really good idea! What kind of tech product do you want to create? And what will it do?

In order to create something that lots of people want or need, you need to be good at **observing, asking questions and listening.**

Speak to your friends and family and ask them if there's anything that would make their lives easier. Is there anything that is **missing in your community?** What might **help your school teacher or classmates?** For example . . .

When seven-year-old Brinda Jain, from India, discovered that ambulances weren't reaching their patients quickly enough in her town, she created an app called Ambulance Whizz. It helps to find a quicker route for ambulances through traffic, helping to save many lives.

When 16-year-old Brandon Boynton, from the USA, was bullied by other children at school, he decided to create an app called BullyBox. It allows children to safely and secretly report bullying to their teachers.

Once you've found your problem, it's time to get creative and start **brainstorming solutions.** You could make a **mind map** to 'map out' your ideas.

A machine that prints books for you at home.

Bad for the environment

A motorbike that delivers books?

profile

Problem:
Granny loves reading printed books but she has broken her leg and can't go to the library.

An app to book the robot

An electric robot that delivers books!

A library app that asks people for help?

location

This is where being good at **working as a team** can be useful. A lot of entrepreneurs like to launch their start-up with another person, known as a **co-founder,** or with a small team. You can often solve problems more easily when you have someone you trust by your side.

Once you've found your idea, it's time to do some **research!** Find out if there is any tech out there that is already solving the problem – you could search online or ask your family, friends and teachers. If no one is already solving the problem, then there is a **gap in the market.**

Now you can start your tech company . . .

HOW DO YOU
LAUNCH A TECH START-UP?

There are many different ways to start a tech company, so it's important to think carefully about how your start-up will work best.

You can move faster when you have a **team of people working together** to create your tech product. Hiring a team of people with different skills and from a **wide variety of backgrounds** is important for a start-up's success.

There are many people involved in a company, from **coders** who tell computers what to do . . .

and **designers** who design the images and information you see on screens . . .

DID YOU KNOW?
The most important person in a company is usually called the **Chief Executive Officer (CEO)** or **Managing Director (MD)**.

to **marketers** who help people find out about your tech product, and **salespeople** who help people buy it.

To build a successful team, you need to have good **leadership** and **communication** skills. It's important that you pay the people who work for your tech start-up fairly and on time, and that you listen to any problems they might have.

But how will you pay for your team? You'll need money to create your tech and hire people. Some entrepreneurs **save up** the money they earn from another job to start their company. Others **raise money** to get started.

You could raise money from **investors.** Investors are people who give money to companies. In exchange, they will own a part of your start-up – if your company is successful, they will be paid back when it grows or is sold.

The best investors will help you with your start-up and **give you advice.**

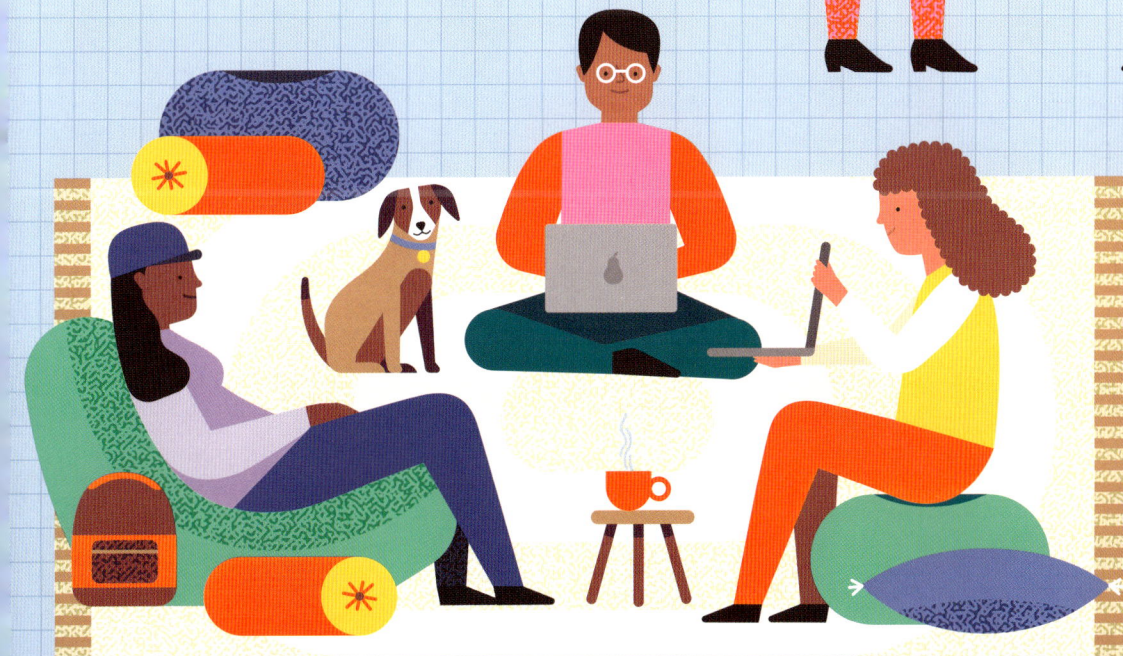

Or you could apply for a **loan** to **borrow money** from the bank, but you will have to pay this back with **interest,** which means that the amount you owe back gets bigger over time.

Or you might decide to raise money from the **public.** This is known as **crowdfunding.**

When you have raised your money and found your team, it's time to create your tech product . . .

HOW DO YOU DESIGN YOUR TECH PRODUCT?

Now it's time to start thinking about what your tech product will look like and how it will work.

A **graphic designer** uses colour, pictures and lettering to make an app or product look fun and exciting.

User Experience (UX) designers work with graphic designers to create products that are easy and enjoyable to use.

Aa Bb Cc Dd Ef Ff Gg
Aa Bb Cc Dd Ef Ff Gg

Industrial designers and **engineers** design the physical products we use, such as phones, games consoles, microwaves, 3D printers and drones.

Wearable tech designers create tech you can wear, such as smart watches that can connect to the internet. The tech needs to be comfortable, fashionable and good at processing a lot of information!

Robotics engineers design and build robots. They have to think about how the robot will move, what shape they should be and what materials they should be made from.

There are many different types of robotics engineers. Some create robots that can explore the depths of the oceans, or be launched into space to find information about other planets!

DID YOU KNOW?
Human-like robots might one day be sent to Mars to explore and build homes before human astronauts arrive.

WHAT DOES A CODER DO?

Your tech product might look good, but it won't be able to do anything without a program. This is where coding comes in . . .

A program (also known as **code**) is what makes a computer play games or music. It's what tells a robot where to go or makes your microwave work. An app is a program.

To create a program, you need to learn how to write code, or hire someone to do it for you. A **coder** creates a **set of instructions** for your computer to follow. It's a bit like the steps you might follow in a recipe to make a cake.

There are many different **computer languages,** which coders use for different things, from making apps to creating websites.

Electronics engineers use code to make the physical parts of your product work, such as making touchscreens respond to different finger movements and deciding what type of battery to use.

Software engineers use code to make the digital parts of your product work, from developing an app for your phone to telling robots how to avoid obstacles.

To create code for a robot, you will have to tell it where to go. Think about your route to school in the morning. Can you write down **every step of the journey?** This list of steps is called an **algorithm!**

Sometimes you might find a **mistake** in your program. This is called a **bug.** Coders spend a lot of time finding and fixing bugs in the code they've written.

DID YOU KNOW?

The first computer bug really was an insect! In 1947, engineers who were fixing a computer found a moth trapped inside!

BOOK ROBOT

I deliver books!

When you have designed your product and created your program, you need to **test your idea** to make sure that it really works for other people. This is called **user testing.**

You put your tech in front of people who might want to use it and **ask them questions** about their experience with it. It's important to listen to your testers and take on board their feedback.

HOW DO YOU GROW YOUR START-UP?

To be successful and make money, your product usually needs to be used by a lot of people as fast as possible.

Once you have launched your tech, how do you get people to hear about it and start using it? Your first few users might be friends and family, but how do you get the next hundred, thousand or even million users? This is where **marketing** comes in.

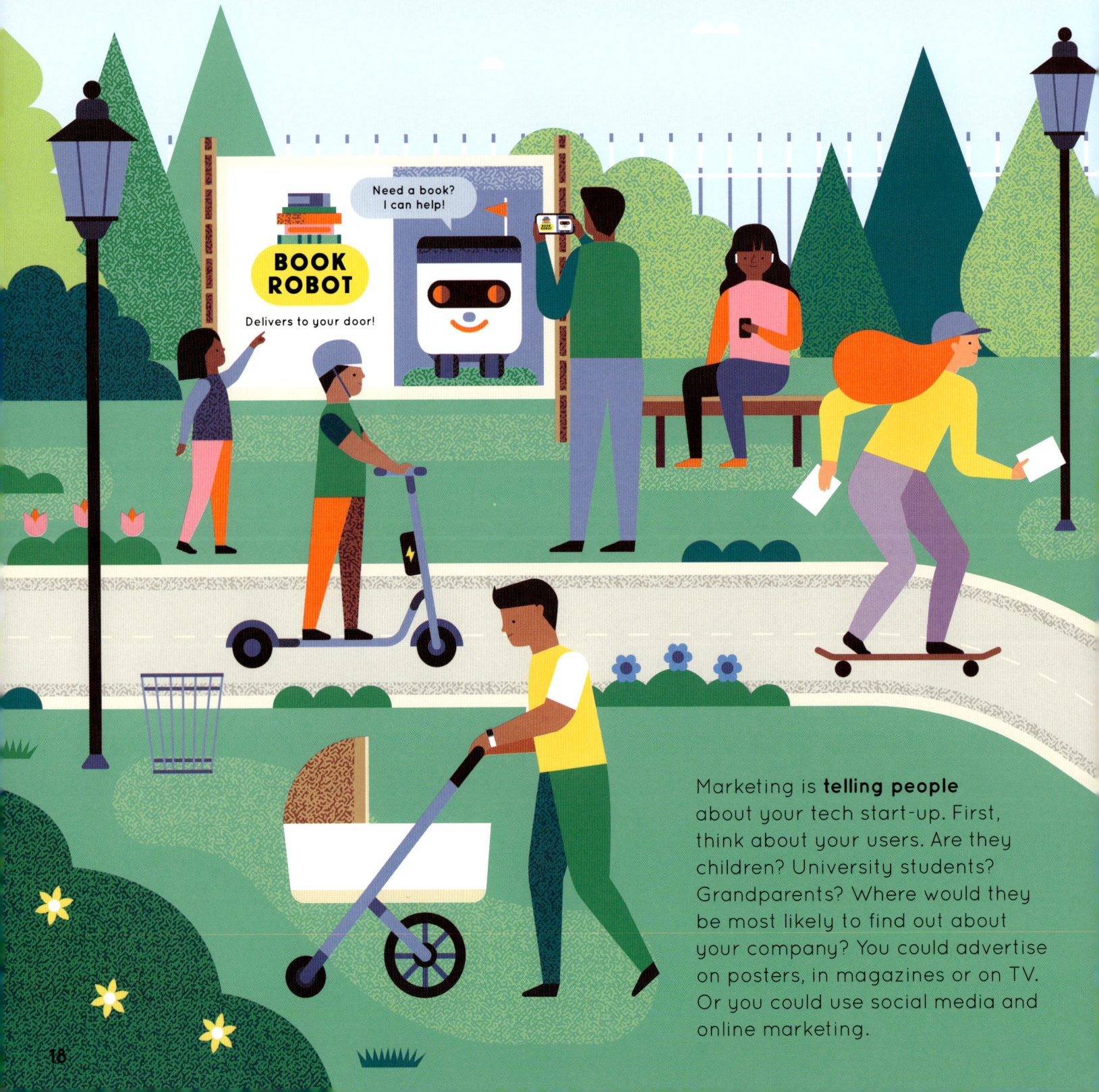

BOOK ROBOT

Delivers to your door!

Need a book? I can help!

Marketing is **telling people** about your tech start-up. First, think about your users. Are they children? University students? Grandparents? Where would they be most likely to find out about your company? You could advertise on posters, in magazines or on TV. Or you could use social media and online marketing.

You can find more customers if you give your start-up an attractive personality. This is known as a **brand.** Imagine that your start-up is a person. Would they be friendly, fun, serious, tough, kind, jokey? It's important to think about your brand at every stage – from your company **name** and **logo** to the writing on your **website.**

DID YOU KNOW?
If a tech company grows extremely quickly and is worth a billion dollars or more, it is known as a **unicorn.**

Once you have users, you can find out how well your start-up is doing by tracking information, known as **data. Data analysts** study data, such as how much money you're making, or how often people are using your tech, and suggest ways to improve your start-up.

BOOK ROBOT
I deliver books!

You need to be willing to **test out ideas** and **change your plan** as you learn more about your customers and how they are using your tech.

19

WHAT HAPPENS WHEN
THINGS GO WRONG?

Launching a tech start-up isn't easy and you are bound to make some mistakes along the way, but the best entrepreneurs are able to stay positive, look for solutions to problems and learn from their failures.

Tech companies can run into all kinds of problems. Some products break or cause accidents. They might even end up being banned in some places.

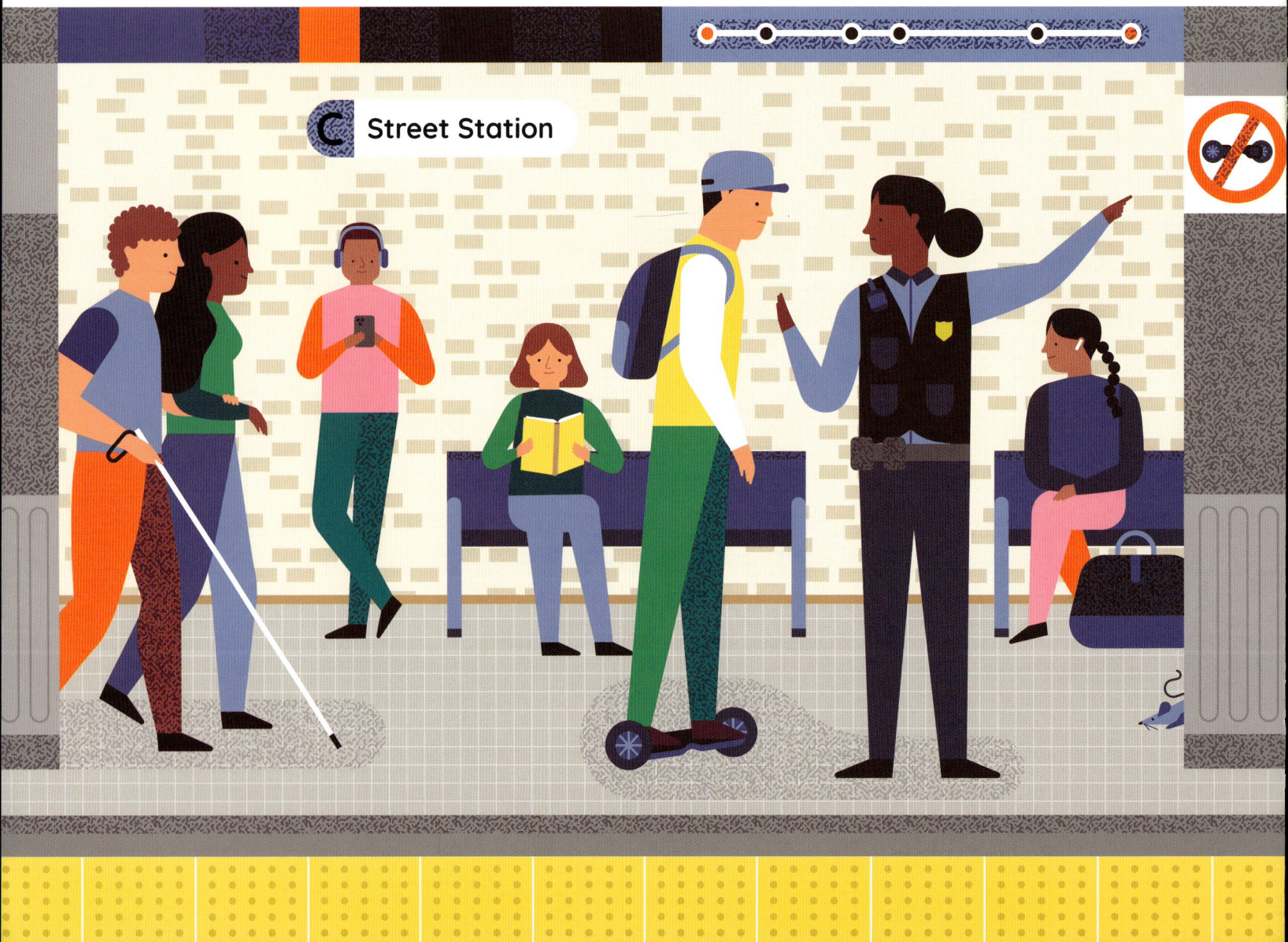

C Street Station

You might **spend too much money** creating your product or building your team. Or you might **not make enough money** because your product isn't being used by enough people. Some investors won't give companies more money if they **don't grow quickly enough.**

The important thing is to **pick yourself up** and **try again.** You can look for lots of **different solutions** to the problem by gathering information and making changes to your product or team. The more solutions you try, the more likely you are to solve your problem.

You will become a stronger entrepreneur if you can be **open-minded,** keep going and **persevere.** Why not practise building these skills now?

Next time you lose a game, fail a spelling test or forget your lines in a play, try not to get upset or angry. Instead, ask yourself . . .

What did I learn from this failure?

How can it help me to grow and improve?

Sometimes, looking for solutions to the problem might lead you to a **completely different idea.** This is called a **pivot.**

You might find that not enough people want to use your robot to borrow books from the library. But that doesn't mean the robot is useless – it could deliver other things too, like groceries.

DELIVERY ROBOT

I deliver to your door!

Almost every successful tech entrepreneur has failed at some point in their life, but if you can learn and grow from your mistakes, or even pivot your company, then you will be on your way to success!

WHAT ABOUT A
JOB IN ARTIFICIAL INTELLIGENCE?

Artificial intelligence (AI) is technology that teaches computers to think and learn the way humans do.

Unlike programming, where a human gives a computer an exact list of instructions to follow, AI is technology that learns what to do by finding patterns in huge collections of information, such as all the text, photos and videos on the internet.

AI can help computers to recognise people's faces from photos and videos, write new content, such as stories, songs and videos, and make complicated decisions.

AI engineers program and train the AI so that it can think and learn like a human.

AI researchers work with scientists and engineers to develop new AI systems and find ways to use AI to overcome problems.

DID YOU KNOW?
AI can play games like you do, such as chess and Minecraft!

AI can also help us discover cures for diseases, create self-driving cars, instantly translate text or speech so we can communicate in different languages, and predict natural disasters like earthquakes and hurricanes.

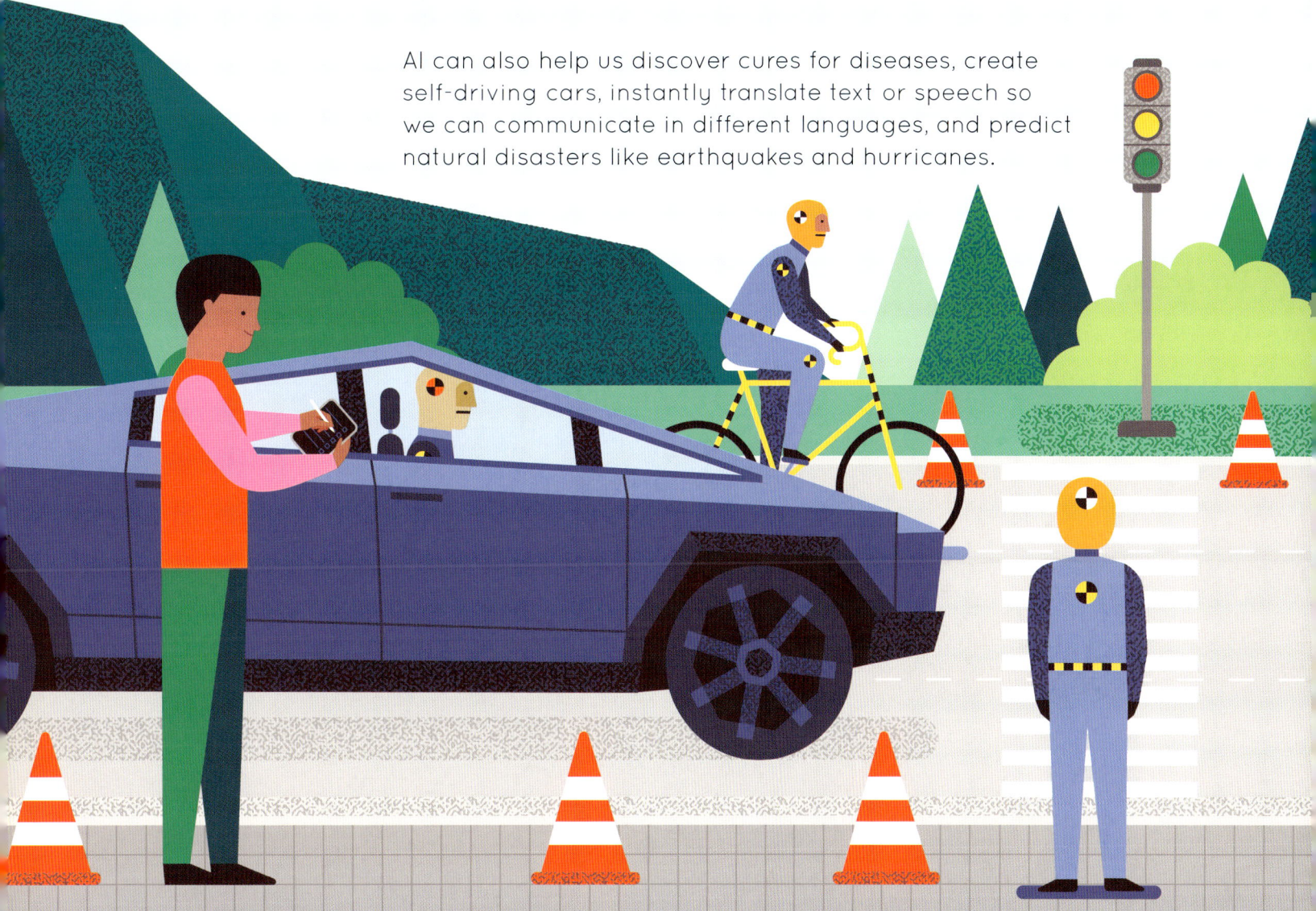

But it is really important to make sure the AI we create is **fair.** AI is trained on collections of content created by humans, who might not want their work to be used by AI and should be allowed to **protect** it.

Some of the content created by humans may also be unfair or unkind to others. This is called **bias.** If AI is going to make decisions for humans, such as who gets hired for a job or whether someone is guilty of a crime, we need to make sure those decisions are fair, and that AI doesn't learn to have any kind of bias.

We also need to make sure that the AI keeps us safe and happy and doesn't accidentally learn to do things we don't want it to do. **Alignment researchers** and **AI safety researchers** are working with governments and companies to make this happen.

DO YOU
LOVE GAMING?
THEN TRY ONE OF THESE JOBS.

You might be surprised to discover that there are hundreds of jobs in the video games industry, from artists to content creators.

Games producers are the people who manage the creation of the game. They raise money, find experts to create the game and help with any problems along the way.

Games designers come up with the look and feel of the video game. They map out what type of game it will be, and work with **games writers** to create the characters and story.

Concept artists create all the early drawings for the game, including the characters and scenery.

Games artists create visuals for the characters, worlds and detail, from spooky dungeons to reflections on windows.

Animators create movement in characters, vehicles and objects, to make the player feel they are inside the world of the game. Some animators use motion-capture technology to record real-life movements of actors and turn them into computer-generated (CG) characters.

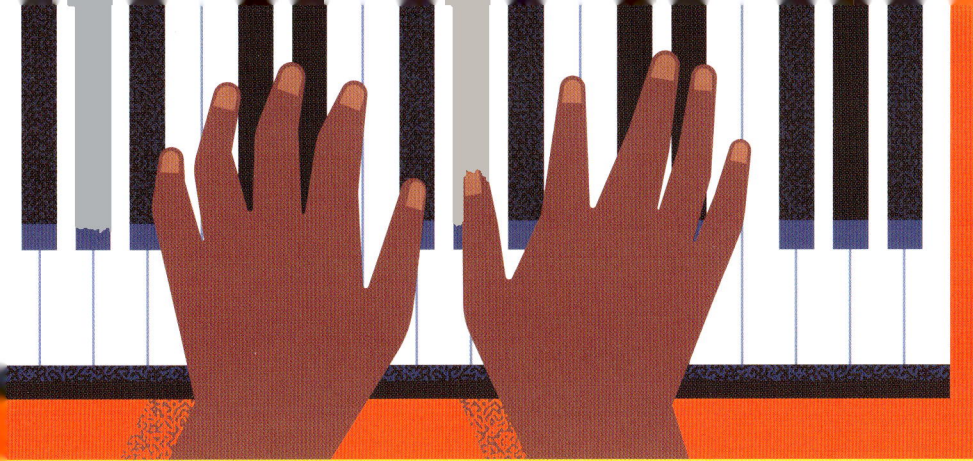

Music composers create music for games, adding excitement or making a scene feel scary.

Sound designers create sound effects, such as rain, footsteps and crashes.

Games software engineers use their coding skills to turn the games designers', artists' and writers' work into a game.

Virtual reality (VR) games are played using a headset that gives you a greater feeling of being in a different world. **VR programmers** write the code for these games.

Augmented reality (AR) programmers code games to show digital images or animations on top of the real world, often using smartphones or tablets with cameras.

DID YOU KNOW?
Video game testers are paid to play video games! They look for problems and suggest ways to improve the game.

Professional gamers are so good at gaming that people pay to watch them play! They might game online, in arenas and even in giant stadiums.

Gaming content creators and **live streamers** create videos of themselves playing or talking about video games.

DO YOU WANT TO
HELP SAVE THE PLANET?
THEN ONE OF THESE TECH JOBS COULD BE FOR YOU.

Climate change is one of the biggest challenges we face today. Almost everything we do, from heating buildings and driving petrol cars to throwing away packaging and food, creates pollution and waste which causes global warming.

But many people are developing tech to tackle the climate crisis . . .

Solar panel and wind turbine engineers create energy from the sun and wind. As the sun shines on solar panels or wind turns a turbine, energy that does not pollute the planet is created. It can be used to light our homes, power our TVs and charge our smartphones.

Aeronautical engineers are working to design aeroplanes that can run on fuel made from plants.

Electric car engineers design and build vehicles that can run on electricity instead of petrol or diesel.

Scientists are developing technology that could give us an unlimited source of energy for everything we need through a process called nuclear fusion.

A lot of land and water are needed to farm animals to eat. Precious forests are chopped down to make room and harmful gases are released. To stop harming animals and the planet, scientists working in **cellular agriculture** use clever technology to create meat grown in labs, using cells taken from real animals.

DID YOU KNOW?
AI is helping researchers find new ways to create lab-grown meat, eggs, milk and fish.

Materials engineers find ways we can use plants, such as seaweed and mango peelings, instead of harmful materials like plastic.

Carbon removal experts take harmful carbon dioxide from the atmosphere and store it somewhere else. Direct air capture is when large fans absorb the pollution and then inject it underground to be stored in rock.

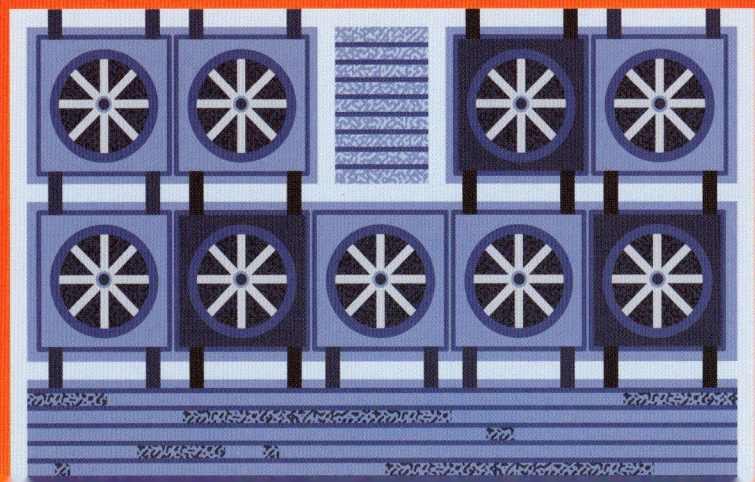

Robotics engineers are developing robotic bees that could be used to pollinate crops and monitor the climate.

DO YOU WANT TO
HELP SAVE LIVES?
THEN TRY ONE OF THESE TECH JOBS.

Robotics engineers develop robots that can help doctors perform life-saving surgery.

They also work with **prosthetists** to design robotic body parts with sensors, motors and batteries for people with missing limbs.

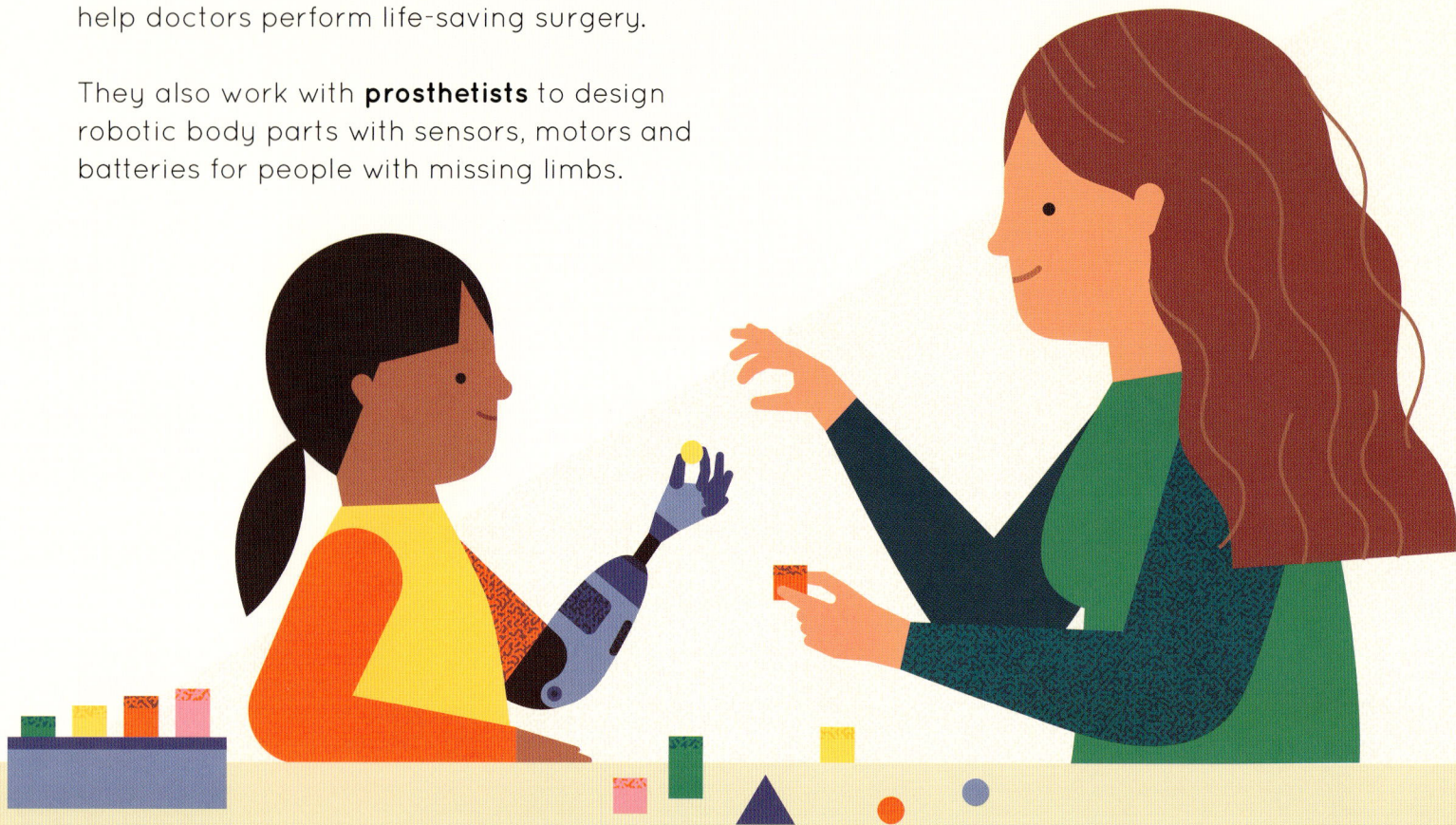

Biomedical engineers create clever machines, implants and devices, such as . . .

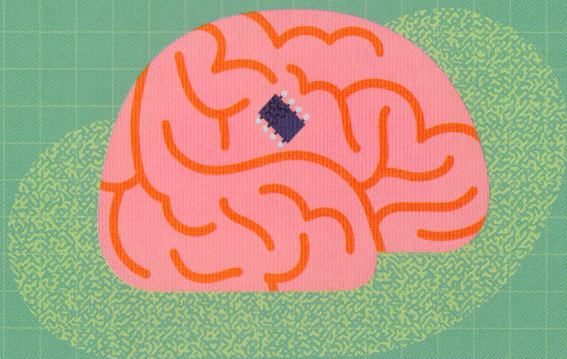

Machines that allow a person with speech or movement difficulties to write or say something using the movement of just their eyes or head.

Brain implants that can help people who are severely paralysed to communicate or use the internet.

Medical research scientists use AI and other technology to help find cures to diseases as well as ways to catch them early before they spread.

Gene therapists use technology to cure diseases. Genes are like codes inside our bodies that decide things like how tall we are or what colour eyes we have. By changing the gene that caused the disease, a person is able to be cured.

Cochlear implants that connect to a nerve in the ear and can help some deaf people to hear.

DID YOU KNOW?
Smartwatches and smart rings can give you all sorts of information about your health, from how fast your heart beats to how well you sleep.

Flash glucose monitors that help people with diabetes to monitor their blood sugar levels.

59

WHAT ABOUT THE
MORE UNUSUAL TECH JOBS?

If you enjoy speaking to people, writing and finding out information, why not become a **tech journalist?** They report on all the latest news in tech.

TECHBRUNCH

TECHBRUNCH

Gadget reviewers are paid to give their opinions about gadgets on social media or blogs, over YouTube or in newspapers and magazines.

If you love fashion, then you could become a **digital fashion designer.** They use computer technology to create clothes for video games, apps, films and virtual worlds.

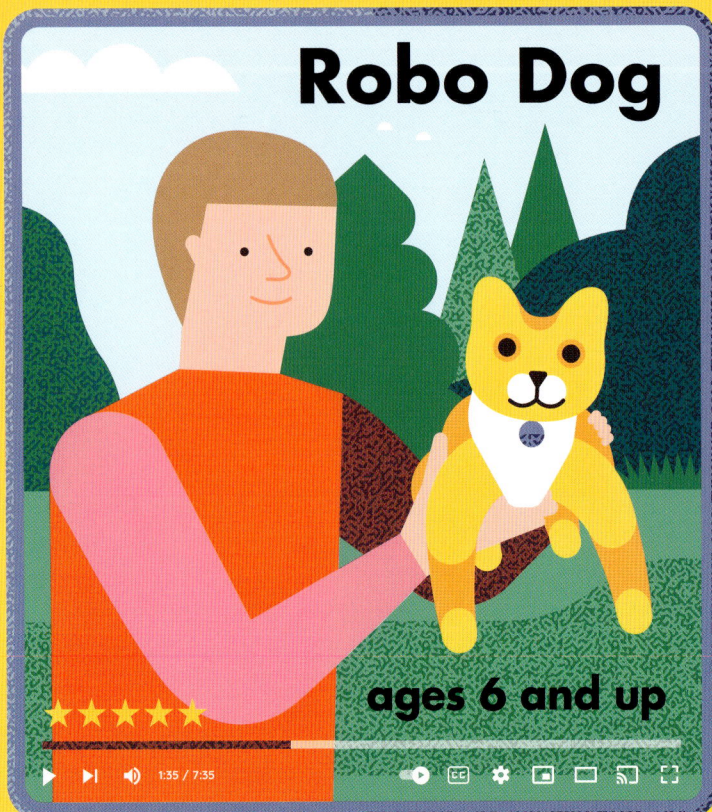

Robo Dog

ages 6 and up

1:35 / 7:35

Do you like telling jokes? **Meme creators** find funny ways to share messages using images and captions. Companies use memes to catch a customer's attention and to give their brand a funny personality.

GOOD MORNING?

I DON'T THINK SO

Ethical hackers keep important computer systems safe and secure from criminals by looking for ways that they could be hacked (broken into).

Everything we do on our computers and online leaves a trace. **Digital forensics specialists** use this digital evidence to catch criminals.

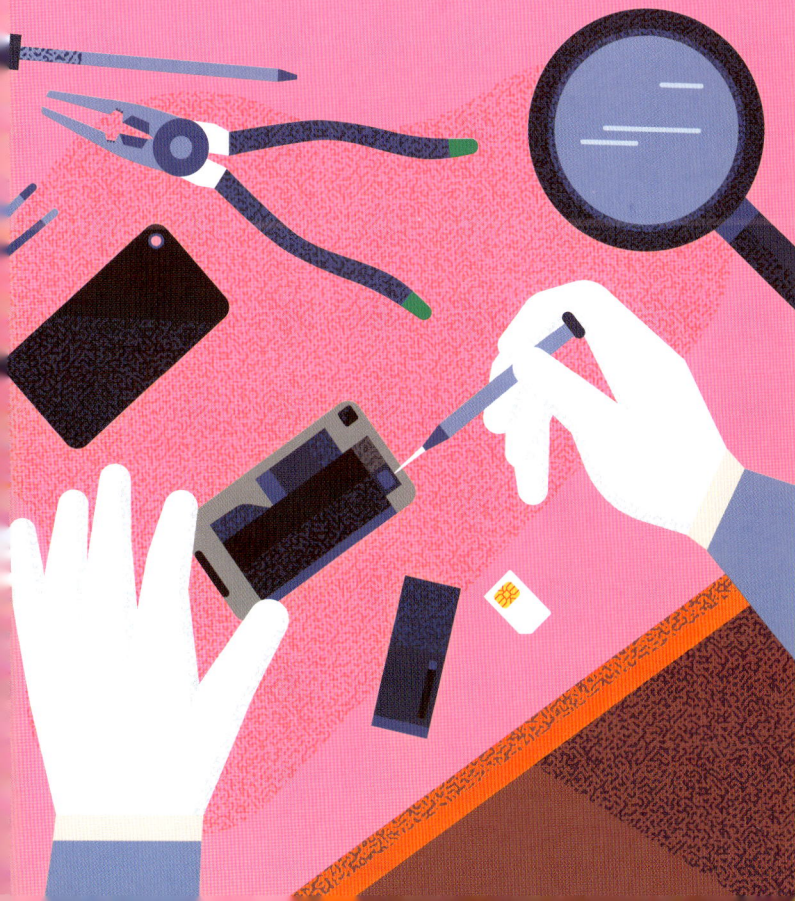

Open-source intelligence researchers are a bit like detectives. They search the Internet using tools like Google Earth to solve crimes.

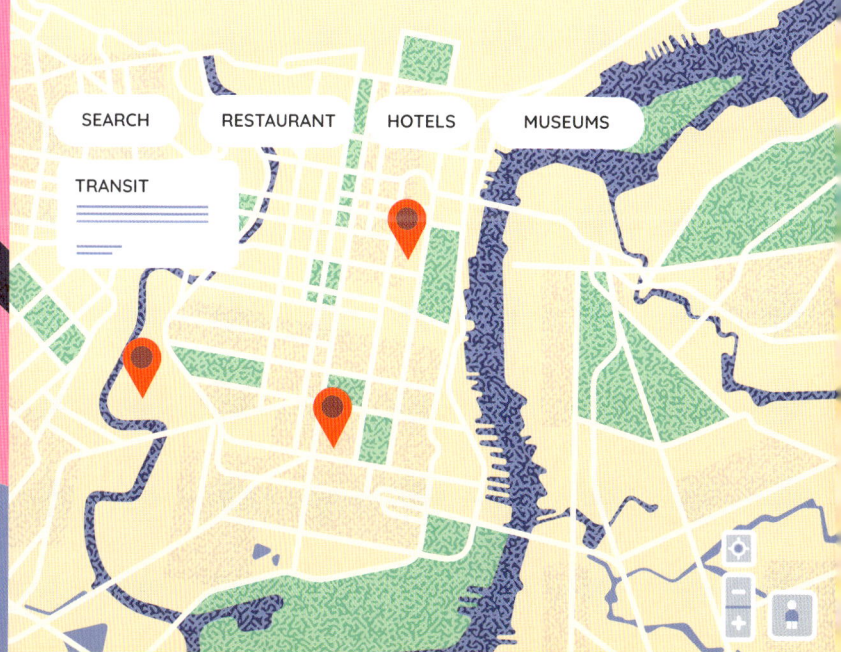

SEARCH   RESTAURANT   HOTELS   MUSEUMS

TRANSIT

Tech jobs will change more and more as technology develops. One day **you** might have a tech job that doesn't even exist yet!

GET INVOLVED!

If you would like to learn more about launching a tech start-up or working in the tech industry, there are many things you can do . . .

Why not join or start a coding club at your school, learn to create your own games online or even start designing a robot?

Sometimes ideas come to you when you least expect them. You could make a list of possible ideas for your tech company, which you can add to any time you think of a new one. And if you don't have an idea yet, don't worry! Keep talking to your friends, family and teachers, and find out what products might help to make their lives easier.

To begin with, all you need is a passion and a curiosity!

USEFUL ORGANISATIONS AND WEBSITES INCLUDE:

ScratchJr. www.scratchjr.org
Code Monster www.crunchzilla.com/code-monster
Raspberry Pi https://projects.raspberrypi.org/en
Studio Code https://studio.code.org/courses
BBC Bitesize Computing www.bbc.co.uk/bitesize/subjects/zvnrq6f
Biz Kids Games https://bizkids.com/games/